FRANZ KAFKA
APPARATUS

FRANZ KAFKA
APPARATUS

ROSS DINWIDDY

DARE DEVIL

bluedeviltheatre.co.uk

FRANZ KAFKA – APPARATUS

First staged at The Rialto Theatre, Brighton
on 4th May 2018 as part of The Brighton Fringe,
with the following cast.

The Officer................Emily Carding
The Condemned Man…....Luis Amália
The Traveller.............Matt Hastings
The Soldier…….....Maximus Polling

Directed by Ross Dinwiddy
Produced by Alex Grace and Rich Bright

SCENE 1

A DESOLATE WASTELAND ON THE EDGE
OF A GAPING PIT

*The set is almost entirely black, the walls draped
with light-consuming black cloth.*

*There is a narrow, high bed made from tarnished,
tubular steel with wheels on the legs - it looks like
the kind of thing used in hospitals for transporting
patients. Its surface is covered in the same black
cloth, there are wrist, neck and ankle restraints
made from thick leather.*

*There is a small, battered, metal table with a leather
document folder, a small pair of white cotton gloves
and a pair of long, gleaming dressmaker scissors.*

Near this, is a single chair, also tarnished metal.

*Present is **The Traveller** - a middle-aged man dressed in a cream linen suit, who is pacing the stage.*

The Officer enters from the back of the theatre and walks through the audience towards the stage. She is a woman of around 40, dressed in a smart, high ranking uniform complete with medals. Incongruous with this, she wears a pair of hand-protecting workman's gloves and carries a pair of long, pointed pliers. Her eyes are protected by a small pair of metal framed goggles.

The Officer It's a remarkable apparatus.

The Officer has reached the stage, she is gazing upwards. She seems to be admiring something in the darkness above the stage, particularly the area over the tubular steel bed with the restraints. (We never see the apparatus; its actual appearance must be left to the audience's imagination.)

The Traveller does not look up, he continues to pace, he seems impatient, distracted.

The Traveller Umm.

The Officer *(Putting down the pliers and taking off the gloves and goggles)* It's all prepared now and ready to go!

The Officer wipes her brow and tucks two dainty, embroidered ladies' handkerchiefs under her collar.

The Traveller *(Stops pacing and looks The Officer up and down)* Those uniforms are really too heavy for this climate.

The Traveller loosens the collar of his shirt with a hooked finger.

The Officer That's true, but they mean home to us, and we don't want to lose touch with our homeland. Now, do have a look at the apparatus. *(She points up to the device)*. Up to this point I've had to do some work by hand, but from now on it should work entirely on its own.

The Traveller nods and politely looks up.

The Officer Of course, breakdowns do happen. I really hope none will occur today, but we must be prepared. The apparatus is supposed to keep going for twelve hours without interruption. But in the event of any breakdowns, they'll only be very minor, and I'll deal with them right away. *(She gestures to the chair)* Don't you want to sit down?

The Traveller glances over his shoulder at the chair.

The Traveller Thank you. *(He sits)*

The Officer I don't know if the Commandant has already explained the apparatus to you.

The Traveller *(Uncomfortably)* I was simply told that there was to be an execution.

The Officer I see. This apparatus is our previous Commandant's invention. I was chosen to work with him on the very first tests and I then took part in all the work right up to its completion. However, all of the credit for its invention belongs to him and him alone. That is inarguable. Have you heard of our previous Commandant?

The Traveller *(Shaking his head indifferently)* No.

The Officer No? Well, I'm not claiming too much when I say that the organisation of this entire penal colony is his work. We, his friends, already knew at the time of his death that the administration of the colony was so self-contained, so self-perpetuating that even if his successor arrived with a thousand new ideas in mind, he would not be able to alter anything of the old system, at least not for several years. And our prediction has held true. The new Commandant has had to recognise that and... *(Pause)* It's a terrible shame that you didn't know the previous Commandant.

The Officer shakes her head and looks disappointedly at The Traveller.

The Traveller shrugs.

The Officer However, I digress. This apparatus essentially consists of three parts. With the passage of time, naturally, certain popular names have been developed for each of these parts. *(She pats the surface of the tubular steel bed with the palms of*

both hands) The one underneath is called the bed,
(She begins to point and gesture at things in the
darkness above the bed) the upper one is called the
inscriber, and here in the middle, that moving part, is
called the harrow.

The Traveller The harrow?

The Officer Yes, the harrow. The name is most apt.
The needles are arranged as in a harrow, and the
whole thing is driven like a harrow, although, in
principle, it is much more artistic. You'll understand
it presently.

The Officer produces a chromatic pitch pipe, adjusts
it carefully to the right note and blows it sharply.

The Soldier *and* **The Condemned Man** *enter, also*
from the back of the theatre. They are both young
men of around 20. The Soldier is holding a heavy
chain which is attached to the shackles of The
Condemned Man. They walk through the audience
and position themselves near the stage.

The Officer The Condemned Man is laid out here on
the bed. First, I'll describe the apparatus and only
then let the procedure go to work. That way you'll be
able to follow it properly. Also, I should point out
that a sprocket in the inscriber is excessively worn. It
really squeaks. When it's in motion one can hardly
make oneself understood. It's intolerable, really.
Unfortunately, replacement parts are difficult to
come by in this place.

The Officer shakes her head with what seems like barely contained rage.

The Officer *(Regathering her composure)* So, here is the bed. The whole thing is covered with a layer of cotton wool, the purpose of which you'll find out in a moment. The Condemned Man is laid out on his stomach on the cotton wool - naked, of course. There are conveniently positioned straps for the hands here, for the feet here, and for the throat here, to tie him in securely. At the head of the bed here, is this small protruding lump of felt, which can easily be adjusted so that it presses right into his mouth. Its purpose is to prevent him screaming and biting his tongue to shreds. Of course, the man has to let the felt into his mouth, otherwise the tight strap around his throat would break his neck.

The Traveller That's cotton wool?

The Officer Yes, it is, feel it for yourself.

The Officer takes The Traveller's hand and leads him from the chair over to the bed.

The Officer It's a specially prepared cotton wool. That's why it looks so completely unrecognisable. I'll get around to mentioning its exact purpose in a moment.

The Traveller now seems a little more interested in the device. He looks up and down between the apparatus and the bed.

*The Condemned Man does the same, almost as if
mimicking The Traveller.*

*The Soldier is standing to attention, but his face
reveals that he is bored and tired.*

The Traveller So now the man is lying down here.
(He pats his hand on the cotton wool)

The Officer Yes, both the bed and the inscriber have
their own electric batteries. The bed needs them for
itself, and the inscriber for the harrow. As soon as
the man is strapped in securely, the apparatus is set
in motion with this.

*She strides over to a heavy industrial looking lever
and touches it gently, almost lovingly.*

The Officer The bed will then start to quiver with
tiny, very rapid oscillations from side to side and up
and down simultaneously. You will have seen
similar devices in mental hospitals. Only with our
bed all movements are precisely calibrated, for they
must be meticulously coordinated with the
movements of the harrow. But it's the harrow which
has the job of actually carrying out the sentence.

The Traveller And what exactly is the sentence?

The Officer *(With astonishment)* You don't even
know that? *(She bites her bottom lip)* Forgive me if
my explanations are perhaps a little jumbled. I really
do beg your pardon. Previously, you see, it was the

Commandant's habit to provide such explanations. But the new Commandant has excused himself from this honourable duty. The very fact that with such an eminent visitor...

The Traveller raises both hands to deflect the complement.

The Officer *(Insisting anyway)* ...that with such an eminent visitor, a distinguished man of letters, he didn't even once make you aware of the form of our sentencing is yet again something new, which...

The Officer is getting visibly irate and agitated, she collects herself and clears her throat.

The Officer In any event, I am without question the person best able to explain our manner of sentencing. For here I am, a woman in possession of all the relevant technical drawings and diagrams, which were entirely conceived and drawn by the previous Commandant.

The Officer strides over to the table and gently rests her hand on the document folder with reverence glistening in her eyes.

The Traveller What are you saying, diagrams made by the Commandant himself? Was this man a combination of everything? Was he a soldier, a judge, engineer, politician and draftsman?

The Officer He was indeed. Chemist and artist too.

Remarkable in all of them.

The Officer picks up the folder and clasps it to her chest. She takes a deep breath, smiling and closing her eyes as she does so.

The Officer *(Opening her eyes and placing the folder back on the table)* Our sentence does not sound that severe. In fact, it is simply this - the law which a condemned man has violated is inscribed on his body with the harrow. This Condemned Man, for instance, *(She points at the Condemned Man)* will have inscribed on his body, 'Honour your superiors.'

The Traveller glances at The Condemned Man.

The Traveller Does he know his sentence?

The Officer No.

The Traveller He doesn't know his own sentence?

The Officer No. It would be useless to give him that information. He will shortly experience it on his own body. He only recently came here from the mainland and is quite unfamiliar with our methods. What we have in mind should prove quite the surprise.

The Traveller *(Confused)* But doesn't he have some general idea that he's been condemned to death?

The Officer Not that either. I am fluent in his language, but he speaks not a word of ours.

The Traveller He doesn't know he's about to be killed? *(Wiping his forehead with his cuff)* Does he know how his defence went?

The Officer He has had no opportunity to defend himself.

The Traveller But he must have had a chance to defend himself.

The Officer The matter stands like this. Here in the penal colony I have been appointed senior judge. In spite of my obvious youth. For I stood at the side of our Old Commandant in all matters of punishment, and I also know the most about the apparatus. The basic principle I use for my decisions is this: Guilt is always beyond a doubt. Other courts could not follow this principle, for they are made up of many heads and, in addition, have even higher courts above them. But that is not the case here, or at least it was not that way with the previous Commandant. It's true that the new Commandant has already shown a desire to get mixed up in my court, but I've succeeded so far in fending him off. And I'll continue to be successful.

The Officer goes over to The Condemned Man and grasps him by the upper arms.

The Condemned Man gives The Officer a warm if somewhat confused smile. He clearly has no idea what The Officer is talking about.

The Officer *(Tuning her head briefly to The Traveller)* You want this case explained. It's simple - just like all of them. *(Looking back to The Condemned Man with an almost friendly smile, still grasping his arms.)* Twenty-four hours ago, a captain laid a charge that this man had been sleeping on duty. For his task is to stand up every time the clock strikes the hour and salute in front of the captain's front door. That's certainly not a difficult duty. On Wednesday night, the captain wanted to check whether he was fulfilling his responsibility. He opened the door on the stroke of two and found him curled up asleep. So, he got his horsewhip and hit him across the face. Now, instead of begging for forgiveness, this man grabbed the captain by the legs, shook him, and cried out, 'Throw down that whip or I'll eat you up.'

The Officer gives The Condemned Man a seemingly playful little shake as she says the last line and then abruptly lets go of him. She turns back to The Traveller, shakes her head and raises her eyebrows.

The Officer Those are the facts. The captain came to me immediately. I wrote up his statement and right after that, the sentence. Then I had the man chained up. It was all very simple. If I had first summoned the man and interrogated him, the result would have been confusion. He would have lied, and if I had been successful in refuting his lies, he would have replaced them with new lies, and so forth. But now I have him, and I won't release him or listen to him. Does that clarify everything?

The Officer gestures to The Soldier who then leads The Condemned man forward. They position themselves near the table facing the audience.

The Officer But time is slipping by. We should be starting the execution, and I haven't finished explaining the apparatus yet.

The Officer returns to the apparatus and points up.

The Traveller seems reluctant to get too near.

The Soldier now looks even more weary and bored.

The Officer As you can see, the shape of the harrow corresponds elegantly to the shape of a man. That is the harrow arrangement for the upper body, and there are the harrows for the legs. This small cutter is the only one designated specifically for the head. Is that all clear to you?

The Traveller looks up at the harrow with a wrinkled frown. Then nods tentatively.

The Traveller Will the Commandant be present at the execution?

The Officer This is not certain. That's why we need to hurry up. As much as I regret the fact, I'll have to make my explanations even shorter. But tomorrow, once the apparatus is clean again, the fact that it gets so very dirty is its only fault, I can sit you down and provide you with the most in-depth explanation of every aspect. But for now, alas, only the most important details.

The Officer stands behind the bed and spreads her arms.

The Officer When the man is lying on the bed and it starts quivering, the harrow sinks onto the body. It positions itself automatically in such a way that it touches the skin only lightly with the needle tips. *(She wiggles her fingers in front of her as if delicately playing a piano)* Once the harrow is in this position, this steel cable tightens up into a rod. And now the performance begins. From the outside, the inexpert eye will see no difference in the punishment at this stage. The harrow seems to do its work uniformly. As it quivers, it sticks the tips of its needles into the body, which is also vibrating from the movement of the bed. Now, to enable someone to check on how the sentence is being carried out, the harrow is made of glass. That gave rise to certain technical difficulties with fastening the needles securely, but after several experimental attempts we were successful. We didn't spare any efforts. And now, as the inscription is made on the body, everyone can see through the glass. Don't you want to come closer and see the needles for yourself?

Hesitantly, The Traveller now moves closer to the bed. He holds his head over it and looks directly upwards.

The Soldier (still holding the chain) is resting

against the table, eyes closed; perhaps he is asleep on his feet.

The Condemned Man pulls on his chain and walks over to the bed. He watches The Officer's gesticulations in regard to the apparatus with smiling, if somewhat puzzled, interest.

The Officer You see, you see, there are two sorts of needles in a multiple arrangement. Each long needle has a short one next to it. The long one inscribes, and the short one squirts water out to wash away the blood and keep the inscription always clear. The bloody water is then channelled here in small grooves and finally flows into these main gutters, and the outlet pipe takes it to the pit.

The Officer runs a finger along the bed's surface as if tracing the exact path the bloody water would take. Finally, she touches a clear plastic tube, amongst the bed's crisscrossing tubular steel - there are speckles of blood in it.

The Traveller and The Condemned Man are now closely following The Officer's gestures, almost mirroring each other.

The Officer seems pleased to have The Traveller's attention but then notices The Condemned Man and seethes. She spots the snoozing Soldier and seethes again. She adjusts the pitch pipe, goes over to The Soldier and blows it sharply into his ear.

The Soldier wakes up with a start and a stumble. He first looks at The Officer and gulps, then he sees that The Condemned Man has dared to move over to the bed. He grasps the chain with both hands and pulls The Condemned Man back.

The Condemned Man falls over backwards and writhes around on the ground. This makes the chain clink and rattle.

The Officer Stand him up!

The Officer becomes impatient with all the fumbling. Together with The Soldier, she drags The Condemned Man to his feet.

The Office Handle him carefully!

The Condemned Man is held upright by the armpits, his feet slipping around on the stage.

The Officer *(Sternly to The Soldier)* Stand him over there!

The Officer helps pull The Condemned Man to the other side of the stage from the table.

The Traveller *(Clearing his throat)* Well, now I know all about it.

The Officer *(Releasing her grip on The Condemned Man and forgetting him)* Except the most important thing.

The Officer takes The Traveller by the arm and guides his attention back to the apparatus.

The Officer *(Pointing up high)* There in the inscriber is the mechanism which determines the movement of the harrow, and this mechanism is arranged according to the diagram on which the sentence is set down. *(She goes over to the table)* I still use the diagrams of the previous Commandant.

The Officer opens the leather folder and looks lovingly at the documents within. She then looks at her hands, examining them. She carefully puts on a small pair of white cotton gloves.

The Officer Unfortunately, and please forgive me, but I cannot allow you to actually handle them. They are the most cherished thing I possess. Sit down, and I'll show you them from this small distance.

The Officer carefully takes a large sheet from the folder, unfolds it and then holds it up.

The Traveller (and audience) can now see an extraordinary diagram. An impossible labyrinth of complex lines drawn in a dense hatch. Around the edges, a thick mass of indecipherable symbols and annotations. The document seems to have the quality of a mind-bending optical illusion etching by Escher but with something of an alchemist's chart about it. The Traveller narrows his eyes and leans forward in his seat. He goes into his pocket and produces a pair of half-moon glasses and puts them on.

The Officer Read it.

The Traveller I can't.

The Officer But it's clear.

The Traveller It's very elaborate, it obviously says something important, but I can't for the life of me decipher it.

The Officer Yes, *(She smiles)*, it could never be called calligraphy for school children. One must study it diligently and at length. And if you did, one day, you too would come to understand it clearly and completely. Of course, it can't in anyway be a simplistic script. You see, it's not supposed to kill right away, but on average over a period of twelve hours. The turning point is set for the sixth hour. There must also be many, many elaborate embellishments surrounding the basic script. The essential script moves around the body only in a narrow belt. The rest of the man's skin is reserved for the decorative, yet meaningful, flourishes.

The Officer gently folds up the document and puts it safely away.

The Officer *(Removing the white gloves)* Can you now appreciate the work of the harrow and the whole remarkable apparatus? I'll switch it on, so you can see how marvellous it is in motion.

The Officer pulls the start-up lever.

The lights dim to blackout. The sound of a terrible machine swells.

The Officer Just look at it!

SCENE 2

A DESOLATE WASTELAND ON THE EDGE OF A GAPING PIT

The lights go up.

The stage is largely as before but now there are a few tins of rice pudding, a spoon and a can opener near the bed.

The Bed has been turned so that the head now points towards the audience.

***The Soldier** and **Condemned Man** are standing to one side. The Condemned Man is still in shackles. The Soldier still holds the end of the chain.*

The Officer is standing on the chair holding a large spanner.

The Traveller is watching her, with his arms folded.

The Officer shrugs and spreads her arms apologetically at The Traveller.

The Officer Now that you have seen the apparatus in operation, all but briefly *(beat)* and with a squeaky wheel. *(She flings the spanner to the ground indignantly)* Do you understand the process?

The Traveller I'm beginning to get the measure of it, yes.

The Officer *(Climbing down from the chair)* When the harrow is finished with the first part of the script on the man's back, the layer of cotton wool rolls and turns the body slowly onto its side to give the needles a new area of skin to work on. Meanwhile the flesh that has been lacerated by the inscription is lying on the cotton wool which, because it has been specially treated, immediately stops the bleeding and prepares the script for a further deepening. As the body continues to rotate, prongs on the edge of the harrow pull the blood-sodden cotton wool from the wounds, discards it into the pit, and the harrow goes to work again, as fresh cotton wool is applied. In this way, it keeps making the inscription deeper for twelve hours. For the first six hours, the condemned man goes on living almost as before. He suffers nothing but pain.

The Officer walks round to the head of the bed.

The Officer After two hours, the felt is removed from his mouth, for by this stage the man has no more energy for screaming.

She points to a small, enamelled bowl, with two curly wires attached.

The Officer Here, warm rice pudding is put in this electrically heated bowl. From this the man, if he feels like it, can help himself to what he can lap up with his tongue. No one passes up this opportunity. I can't think of a single one, and I've had a lot of experience. He loses his pleasure in eating around the sixth hour. I usually kneel down at that point to observe the phenomenon. The man rarely swallows the last bit. He turns it around in his mouth and spits it out. When he does that, I have to quickly dodge aside or else he'll get me in the face. *(She strides over to The Condemned Man)* But how quiet the man becomes around that sixth hour! *(She rests her arm around The Condemned Man's shoulders)* Even the most stupid of them begin to understand. It starts around the eyes and spreads out from there. A look that could tempt one to lie down under the harrow one's self. The man simply and beautifully begins to decipher the inscription. You've seen that it's not easy to comprehend the inscription with your eyes, but our man deciphers it with his wounds. True, it takes a lot of work. As I say, it requires six hours to get there, but when it does…

The Officer seems to have drifted into a memory, she falls silent. Then, suddenly, she notices The Traveller's slightly puzzled expression. She snaps herself out of it.

The Officer But anyway, the harrow eventually spits him right out and throws him into the pit, where he splashes down into the bloody water and spent cotton wool. The judgment is over, and we, this Soldier and I, quickly bury him.

The Officer signals The Soldier, again by adjusting and then blowing the pitch pipe.

The Traveller is standing with his hands in his jacket pockets, he dodges aside as the Soldier drags The Condemned Man towards the apparatus.

The Soldier removes the chains and shackles from The Condemned Man's arms, legs and neck. He then takes the large pair of scissors from the table and uses them to cut through The Condemned Man's clothing.

The Condemned Man is stripped and laid out under the harrow on the bed.

The Soldier begins to fasten the restraints – five leather straps with buckles attached to the bed frame. Whilst The Soldier is busy with the right hand, The Condemned Man stretches out his left, pointing to where The Traveller is standing.

The Officer examines The Traveller's reaction, her eyes fixed on him.

The Soldier moves to The Condemned Man's left arm and pulls it into position. As he buckles it down the leather strap breaks.

The Traveller reacts with a concerned frown to the broken strap.

The Officer sees The Traveller's reaction and narrows her eyes. She then dashes across and snatches the torn leather strap from The Soldier and examines it.

The Officer *(Glancing back at The Traveller)* The machine is very complicated. Now and then something is bound to tear or break. One shouldn't let that detract from one's overall opinion. Anyway, we have an immediate replacement for the strap. I'll use a wrist shackle - even though that will affect the sensitivity of the movements for the left arm.

The Officer goes amongst the shackles and chains, which are lying on the stage in a heap, and begins to rummage.

The Officer Our resources for maintaining the apparatus are very limited at the moment. Under the previous Commandant, I had free access to a cash box specially set aside for this purpose. There was a store room here in which all possible replacement parts were kept.

She finds the handcuffs and returns to the bed.

The Officer I admit I made almost extravagant use of it. But that was then, not now, the new Commandant has seen to that.

She clamps The Condemned Man's left wrist to the tubular steel of the bed with the handcuffs.

The Officer For him everything serves only as a pretext to fight against the old arrangements. Now he keeps the cash box under his own control, and if I ask him for a new strap, he demands to see the torn one as a piece of evidence.

The Officer and The Soldier set about adjusting the straps and precisely positioning The Condemned Man's body. The Traveller watches in concerned silence, deep in thought.

The Officer Then the new strap doesn't arrive for ten days, and I insist on this superior brand, which is apparently difficult to justify. How I am supposed to get the apparatus to work properly in the meantime without a strap, no one seems concerned about that.

The Officer forces the wedge of felt into The Condemned Man's mouth.

The Condemned Man struggles, convulses and then vomits. The vomit splatters over the bed frame and onto the stage.

The Officer reacts with horror to the puddle of sick.

The Officer This is all the Commandant's fault!
This is intricate machinery not a sewer.

*With trembling hands, The Officer brings The
Traveller closer to show him what has happened.*

The Officer Haven't I spent hours trying to make
the Commandant understand that from a day before
the execution there should be no more food served?
Oh, but this new lenient, progressive administration
has a different opinion. Before the man is led away,
the Commandant's women cram sugary niceties
down his throat. Look at him, his whole life he's fed
himself on stinking fish, but now, today of all days,
he has to eat huge, cream filled, chocolate coated
eclairs *(Glancing at the puddle of vomit and
narrowing her eyes)* and macaroons too!

*The Traveller's stomach turns, he takes a step
backwards.*

The Officer *(Noticing The Traveller's disgust.)* But
that would be all right - I'd have no objection, but
why won't they get me some fresh felt. I've been
asking them for three months now? Three months!
How can anyone take that felt into his mouth without
feeling disgusted. I mean, something that a hundred
men have sucked and bitten and slobbered over as
they lay there dying?

The Condemned Man has rested his head down and

appears peaceful.

The Officer puts her arm around The Traveller's shoulders, who goes to step even further away. But The Officer grasps him and leads him to one side.

The Officer *(Calling over to The Soldier)* Don't just stand there, do something about that revolting mess!

The Soldier springs to attention. He looks around and spots The Condemned Man's slashed shirt. He quickly begins cleaning up the vomit using the shirt.

The Officer *(She waits and watches for a moment until The Soldier is fully occupied with the task, then...)* I'd like to speak a few words to you in confidence. May I do that?

The Traveller Of course.

The Traveller then listens with his eyes lowered.

The Officer This process and execution, which you are currently having the opportunity to admire, has no more open supporters in our colony. I am its only defender, just as I am the single advocate for the legacy of the Old Commandant.

The Traveller looks up slowly. He glances nervously at The Officer.

The Officer I can no longer plan for, or even contemplate, a more extensive organisation of this process. I'm using all my powers to maintain what there is at present. When the Old Commandant was alive, the colony was full of his supporters. I don't think I flatter myself too much by saying I have something of the Old Commandant's power of persuasion, but I lack his complete autonomy, and as a result our supporters have gone into hiding. There are still a lot of them, I believe that, but no one wants to admit it. If you go into a tea house today - that is to say, on a day of execution - and keep your ears open, perhaps you'll hear nothing but ambiguous remarks. They are all supporters, I know they are, but under the new Commandant, considering his present views, they are totally useless to me. And now I'm asking you: Should such a life's work, *(She points to the apparatus.),* come to nothing because of this Commandant and the women influencing him? Should people stand back let that happen? Even if one is a foreigner and only on our island for a few days? But there's no time to lose. I suspect that there are those already preparing measures against my judicial proceedings. Discussions are always taking place in the Commandant's headquarters, to which I'm never invited, incidentally. Even your visit today seems to me typical of the whole situation. People are cowards and send you out, a foreigner.

The Officer takes her arm from around The Traveller's shoulders and walks to centre stage.

The Traveller watches her intently.

The Officer You should have seen the executions in

the old days! This entire place was overflowing with happy people, they'd start arriving a day before the execution. They all came merely to watch. Early in the morning the Commandant would appear with his women. Glorious fanfares woke up the entire community. I would deliver the news that everything was ready.

The Soldier has finished cleaning up. He stands holding the filthy shirt, which is now dripping with vomit. He looks puzzled as to what to do with it.

The Officer Then everyone, including every high official, had to attend. They would all arrange themselves around the apparatus which would be freshly cleaned and gleaming.

The Soldier shrugs and tosses the vomit soaked shirt to the back of the stage with a splat.

The Officer For almost every execution I had brand new replacement parts, of the finest quality.

The Officer gazes into the distance with tears in her eyes.

The Officer Picture it, all taking place in front of countless admiring eyes. The condemned man stripped and laid down under the harrow by the Commandant himself. What nowadays is done by a common soldier was then my job as the senior judge, and it was an honour for me.

The Soldier takes a tin opener and begins opening one of the tins of rice pudding.

The Officer And then the execution began! No discordant note disturbed the work of the machine. Many people did not look any more at all, but lay down with closed eyes on the ground. They all knew: now justice was being carried out. In silence, people listened to nothing but the groans of the condemned man, muffled only by the felt. These days the machine no longer manages to squeeze a strong, resonating groan out of the condemned man - something the felt is incapable of smothering. But back then, the needles which made the inscription dripped a caustic liquid which we are not permitted to use any more.

The Officer returns to standing next to The Traveller. She still seems to be in a world of her own. She puts her arm around The Traveller's waist.

The Officer Well, then came the sixth hour. It was impossible to grant all the requests people made to be allowed to watch from up close. The Commandant, in his wisdom and kindness, would arrange for the little children to be taken care of before all the rest and given the best view. Naturally, I was always allowed to observe from as closely as I liked, because of my official position.

The Officer squeezes The Traveller close and points to the area immediately in front of the bed, which is still damp from mopping up the vomit.

The Soldier is crouching there, spooning rice pudding into the small bowl in front of The Condemned man's face.

The Officer Often, I crouched down there with two small cherubs in my arms. How we all took in the expression of transfiguration on the martyred face! How we held our cheeks in the glow of this justice, finally attained yet already passing away! True beauty is always so fleeting.

The Officer rests her head on The Traveller's shoulder.

The Officer What times we had, my friend, what times!

The Traveller now looks extremely embarrassed and uncomfortable. Impatiently he pulls away. The Officer is too preoccupied to notice his discomfort.

The Soldier has filled the bowl with rice pudding and stands up straight. The Condemned Man immediately begins lapping at this with his tongue.

The Soldier *(Pushing The Condemned Man's head away from the bowl)* Stop it, stop it!

The Officer *(Finally noticing The Traveller's concerned expression)* I didn't want to upset you in any way. I know it's impossible to make someone understand those days now. Besides, the apparatus still works and operates on its own. It operates on its own even when it is standing alone here. And at the end, the bodies still keep falling in that incredibly elegant flight into the pit, even if hordes of spectators are not gathered around like swarming wasps as they once did.

The Traveller glances around, attempting to avoid eye contact. But The Officer grabs his hands.

The Officer Do you see the shame of it?

The Traveller says nothing.

The Condemned Man seems to be sneaking rice pudding every time The Soldier is not looking.

The Officer lets go of The Traveller and turns round quickly. She turns back with her hands on her hips and a friendly smile on her face.

The Officer *(Cheerfully)* Yesterday I was nearby when the Commandant invited you. I heard the invitation. I know this Commandant. I understood right away what he had in mind. Although his power might be sufficiently great to take action against me, he doesn't yet dare to. He thinks he's exposing me to the judgment of a highly respected foreigner. He calculates things with care and cunning.

The Officer leads The Traveller over to the table. The Traveller sits in the chair, The Officer perches on the table's edge.

The Officer You are now only in your second day on the island. You didn't know the Old Commandant and his way of thinking. You are trapped in a European way of seeing things. Perhaps you are even fundamentally opposed to the death penalty in general and to this style of mechanically achieved execution in particular. Moreover, you have observed that the execution is turning out to be something of a gloomy occasion, without any obvious public participation or enthusiasm, and all done utilising a partially damaged apparatus. Now, if we take all this together - so the Commandant thinks - surely one might easily imagine that you would end up considering my procedure to be… ummm… let's just say, improper? And if you didn't consider it right, you wouldn't keep quiet about it. Oh, no.

The Officer studies The Traveller's expression for a moment.

The Officer I'm still speaking the mind of the Commandant, you understand. I'm certain that you have seen many exotic practices among many peoples around the world and have learned to respect them. Thus, you will probably not speak out against the procedure with your full power, as you would perhaps in your own homeland. But the Commandant doesn't really need that. A casual word, merely a careless remark, is enough. It doesn't have to match your convictions at all, so long as it corresponds to his wishes. I'm certain he will use all his shrewdness to interrogate you. And his women will sit around in a circle and prick up their ears.

You will say something like, 'Among us the judicial procedures are different,' or 'With us the accused is questioned before the verdict,' or 'We had torture only in the Middle Ages.'

The Soldier checks the bowl, lots of the rice pudding has vanished. He turns his back to get the rest of the tin. The Condemned Man uses to opportunity to lap up the rest of the bowl.

The Officer For you these observations appear as correct as they are self-evident – innocent remarks which do not impugn my procedure. But how will the Commandant take them? I can just see him now, our esteemed Commandant, the way he'll immediately push his stool aside...

The Officer jumps to her feet.

The Soldier returns to the bowl to find it virtually empty. There is not enough left in the open tin to fill it to the correct level. He scoops some in anyway.

The Officer ...the way he'll hurry out onto the balcony. I see his women, how they'll scurry after him. I can hear his voice, what those women call his thunderous voice. And now he's speaking: 'A highly respected personality representing the world's press has just said that our process based on old customs is inhuman, barbaric. After this verdict, from such a personality it is, of course, no longer possible for me to tolerate this procedure. So, from this day on I am ordering...' and so forth.

The Officer sits back down on the edge of the table.

The Soldier is opening a second tin of rice pudding.

The Officer You want to intervene - you didn't mean what he's reporting - you never called my procedure inhuman, barbaric; on the contrary, in keeping with your piercing insight, you consider it utterly humane and worthy of the most sophisticated people. You also deeply admire this intricate and ingenious equipment. But it's too late. You don't even go after him out onto the balcony, it's already too crammed with those gibbering women. You want to attract attention. You want to cry out. But a lady's hand is covering your mouth, and with that moment, all the Old Commandant's work is lost, gone like a forgotten dream.

The Traveller *(Suppressing a smile)*. You're exaggerating my influence. The Commandant has read my letters of introduction. He knows that I'm no expert in judicial processes. If I were to express an opinion, it would be that of a lay person, no more significant than the opinion of anyone else. And in any case, far less significant than the opinion of the Commandant himself. Who, as I understand it, has very extensive powers in this penal colony. If his views of this procedure are as definite as you think they are, then I'm afraid the time has probably come for this procedure to end, without any need for my humble opinion.

The Officer shakes her head vigorously, then moves

in close on The Traveller.

The Condemned Man and the Soldier, are now both eating the rice pudding. The Soldier has taken to spooning it into the demanding open mouth of The Condemned Man.

The Officer You don't know the Commandant. As far as he, and all of us, are concerned you are, if you will forgive the expression, to a very large extent innocent. Your influence, believe me, cannot be overestimated. In fact, I was blissfully happy when I heard that you were to be present at the execution by yourself. This order of the Commandant was aimed at me, but now I'll turn it to my advantage. Without being distracted by false insinuations and disparaging looks, which could not have been avoided with a greater number of spectators. You have listened to my explanation, looked at the marvellous apparatus, and you are now about to view the execution itself. Your verdict is no doubt already fixed. If any small uncertainties remain, witnessing this man's sublime death will dispel them. And now I'm asking you, help me deal with the Commandant!

The Traveller How on earth can I do that? It's totally impossible.

The Officer You could do it, *(clenching her fists at her sides).* You could do it! I have a plan which must succeed. You think your influence is insufficient. I know it will be enough. But even assuming you're right, doesn't saving this whole procedure require

one to at least try, even by methods which may at
first appear hopeless? So, listen to my plan. Listen.

They make firm eye contact with each other.

The Officer To carry it out, it's necessary, above all,
for you to keep as quiet as possible today in the
colony about your verdict on this procedure. Unless
someone asks you directly, you should not express
any opinion whatsoever. But what you do say must
be short and vague. People should notice that it's
problematic for you to speak about the subject, that
you feel bitter, that, if you were to speak openly,
you'd not be able to control yourself, you'd have to
burst into a tirade of profanity. I'm not asking you to
lie, not at all. You should only give brief answers.
Something like, 'Yes, I've seen the execution' or
'Yes, I've heard the full explanation.' That's all,
nothing further. For that will be enough of an
indication for people to observe in you a certain
bitterness, even if that's not what the Commandant
will think. Naturally, he will completely
misunderstand the issue and interpret it in his own
way. My plan hinges on that.

The Traveller I really don't understand what you're
asking.

The Officer Allow me to finish, and you will.
Tomorrow a large meeting of all the higher
administrative officials takes place at headquarters
under the chairmanship of the Commandant. He, of
course, understands how to turn such a meeting into

a spectacle. A gallery has been built, which is always full of spectators. I'm compelled to take part in the discussions, though they fill me with disgust. In any case, you will certainly be invited to the meeting. If you follow my plan today and behave accordingly, the invitation will become an emphatic request.

The Traveller Nobody's mentioned any meeting to me yet.

The Officer They will. But should you for some inexplicable reason not be invited, you must make sure you request an invitation. Then you'll receive one without question. Now, tomorrow you are sitting amongst those women in the Commandant's box. With frequent upward glances, he reassures himself that you are there. After various trivial and ridiculous agenda items, designed merely to pander to the audience, this will be mostly harbour construction, always harbour construction, bloody harbour construction, the judicial process will come up for discussion. If it's not raised by the Commandant himself or does not occur soon enough, I'll make sure it does. I'll take the stand and report on today's execution. Really briefly, just an outline summary. Such a report is not really required or even expected; however, I'll do it, nonetheless. The Commandant thanks me, with his usual friendly, false smile. And now he cannot restrain himself. He seizes this excellent opportunity. 'The report of the execution,' he'll say, or something like that, 'has just been given. I would like to add to this report only the fact that this particular execution was attended by the esteemed journalist whose visit confers such extraordinary honour on our colony, as you all know. Even the gravitas of our meeting today has been increased by his very presence. Should we not now ask this renowned writer for his appraisal of the execution?' Of course, this is met with the sound of applause from everywhere, universal, rapturous applause. And I'm louder than anyone. The Commandant bows before you and says, 'Then in everyone's name, I'm putting the question to you.' And now you step up to the railing. Place your hands where everyone can see them. Otherwise those blasted ladies will grab them and play with your fingers. And now finally come your remarks. I don't know how I'll bear the tension up 'til then. In your speech, you mustn't hold back. Let truth resound. Lean over the railing and shout it out! Yes, yes, roar your opinion at the Commandant, your unshakeable opinion!

The Officer examines The Travellers rather alarmed expression.

The Traveller Look, can I just stop you there…

The Officer *(Interrupting)* But perhaps you don't want to do that. It doesn't suit your character. Perhaps in your country people behave differently in such situations. That's all right. That's perfectly understandable. Don't stand up at all. Just say a couple of words. Whisper them so that only the officials underneath you can just about hear them. That's enough. You don't even have to say anything at all about the lack of attendance at the execution or about the squeaky wheel, the torn strap, the disgusting felt. No. I'll take over all further details, and, believe me, if my speech doesn't chase him out of the room, it will force him to his knees, so he'll have to admit it: 'Old Commandant, I bow down before you.' That's my plan. Do you want to help me carry it out? But, of course you want to. More than that, you love it, don't you?

The Officer is gripping The Traveller by both elbows, glaring into his eyes and breathing heavily into his face.

The Traveller *(Emphatically)* No.

The Soldier and The Condemned Man stop eating the rice pudding and, still chewing, look over at The Traveller.

The Officer's blinks several times, but she does not take her eyes off The Traveller.

The Traveller Would you like an explanation?

The Officer nods dumbly.

The Traveller I am absolutely opposed to this procedure. Even before you took me into your confidence (and, of course, I will never abuse your confidence under any circumstances) I was already thinking about whether I was entitled to intervene against it and whether my intervention could have the smallest chance of success. And if that was the case, it was clear to me whom I had to turn to first of all, naturally, to the new Commandant. You have clarified the issue for me even more, but without reinforcing my decision in any way - quite the reverse. I find your conviction genuinely moving, I do, even if it cannot possibly deter me.

The Officer turns quietly and slowly toward the machine, she staggers a few steps forward. She leans back a little, looking up at the inscriber as if she is checking that everything is in order.

The Soldier and The Condemned Man seem to have made friends. The Condemned Man makes a sign to The Soldier with his hands, although, given the tight straps on him, this is a struggle for him to do. The Soldier leans in closely to him. The Condemned Man whispers something. The Soldier nods, smiles warmly and whispers something back. They both chuckle. Then The Soldier gently brushes a few strands of damp hair from The Condemned Man's face. They smile at each other.

The Traveller takes a few steps and stands just behind The Officer, who is still looking up at the apparatus.

The Traveller You don't yet know what I intend to do. I will indeed tell the Commandant my opinion of the procedure, not in a public meeting, but in private. I won't be attending this meeting in the morning under any circumstances.

The Officer *(Not turning to face The Traveller)* So the process has not convinced you.

The Officer finally turns to face The Traveller and a smile develops on her face.

The Officer Then the time has come.

The Traveller *(Uneasily)* Time for what?

But there is no answer.

The Officer *(Turning to The Soldier)* Set him free.

The Soldier says nothing, he looks puzzled.

The Officer I said set him free.

Suddenly The Soldier looks delighted, he hurriedly begins to unbuckle the restraints on The Condemned Man's arms.

The Officer You're tearing my straps, be careful!

The Officer goes over, pushes The Soldier aside and carefully undoes the remaining restraints.

The Soldier rolls his eyes.

With the straps all unbuckled, The Condemned Man simply lies there, he looks questioningly from The Soldier to The Officer to The Traveller, then back to The Soldier.

The Soldier again whispers something to The Condemned Man. They look at each other smiling. The Soldier nods and The Condemned Man's smile gets ever broader.

The Officer Help him off of there.

The Soldier puts his arms around The Condemned Man's naked body and helps him off the bed.

The Officer has returned to the table. She opens the document folder and sorts through the pages. She takes out a document, unfolds it and holds it up. Again, it is a maze of dense lines and confusing symbols crammed onto a large sheet.

The Officer Read that.

The Traveller I can't.

The Officer You can, look.

The Traveller I've already told you, I can't read these things.

The Officer But take a close look at the script.

The Traveller again puts on his glasses and bends in close to the thick hatch of lines.

Nervously, The Officer edges the paper back a little. This document must not be touched.

After a few seconds of study, The Traveller

straightens up, shrugs and shakes his head.

The Officer 'Be just!' it states. Now you can read it.

The Traveller looks back to the paper and narrows his eyes. He shrugs again.

The Officer 'Be just!' it says.

The Traveller That could be it, I suppose.

The Traveller glances at The Officer's expectant face.

The Traveller Umm… I do believe that is written there. Yes… I suppose.

The Officer Good. This sentence will be fed into the inscriber.

The Soldier and The Condemned Man are keeping each other busy. They have found The Condemned Man's trousers. The Condemned Man puts them on with The Soldier's help, they laugh and play as they do so. The slashed trousers won't stay up at first, The Soldier finds a piece of string which The Condemned Man uses as a belt.

The Officer begins to unbutton her jacket. As she does this, the two ladies' handkerchiefs, which she had pushed into her collar, fall away.

The Officer *(To The Condemned Man)* Here, have your handkerchiefs back.

The Officer picks up the two heavily embroidered, lacy handkerchiefs and tosses them in the direction of The Condemned Man.

The Officer *(To The Traveller)* Presents from the Commandant's Women.

The Officer continues to undress. She removes her jacket, brushes the shoulders and lapels with her hand, then folds it carefully and places it on the chair.

The Soldier snatches the handkerchiefs away from The Condemned Man, who attempts to snatch them back. The Soldier teases him with them as they dodge about.

The Officer removes her trousers and examines the creases. Again, she neatly folds them and places them on the chair.

The Soldier and The Condemned Man are now play fighting, wrestling about and laughing. The handkerchiefs dropped to the ground and ignored.

The Officer is now naked. She picks up the neat bundle of her clothes from the chair and throws them at the back of the stage, to where the pit would be. She then goes and spreads herself out, face down on the bed.

The Soldier and The Condemned Man are now holding each other close in an embrace. They are kissing passionately.

The Officer looks across at them with a blank expression.

The Officer You two, stop that and strap me in!

The Soldier and The Condemned Man stop kissing and step apart. The Soldier looks uncertain, he glances between The Officer and The Condemned Man. He slowly approaches the bed and tentatively begins to buckle the straps.

The Condemned Man sees this and excitedly dashes over to join in strapping The Officer down. When they are finished with the straps for the legs and arms...

The Officer Now, start up the apparatus!

The Condemned Man fastens the strap around The Officer's neck but does not force the wedge of felt into her mouth.

The Soldier is hesitant, frightened to even touch the lever. He looks away from The Officer to the Traveller, then to The Condemned Man.

The Traveller seems stunned and paralysed.

The Condemned Man nods his head enthusiastically, encouraging the Soldier.

The Officer Follow your orders, man! Start up the

apparatus!

The Soldier gulps, looks back to the enthusiastically nodding Condemned Man then hesitantly takes hold of the lever. He shakes his head in disbelief, then firmly pulls the lever down.

The lights dim to blackout. The sound of a terrible machine swells.

SCENE 3

A DESOLATE WASTELAND ON THE EDGE
OF A GAPING PIT

*In the darkness, the noise of the machine becomes
more and more frenzied. Then there is thunderous,
frantic crashing and banging. The sound of
destruction. Then... Flash, bang, smoke!*

*As the lights go up, we see that the tubular steel bed
with the restraints and The Officer have gone.*

The stage is more shadowy than before. **The
Traveller, The Soldier** *and* **The Condemned Man**
are staring out over the audience.

The Traveller is standing next to a suitcase, it is adorned with stickers from around the world, indicating a well-travelled man.

The Soldier and The Condemned Man have their arms around each other's waist.

The Traveller *(Turning to The Soldier, clearly distraught)* What the hell went wrong? To begin with it seemed to be working exactly as in the demonstration.

The Soldier releases his arm from The Condemned Man's waist and takes out a tobacco tin and some rolling papers. He begins to roll a cigarette.

The Soldier Yes, then I remembered that the wheel should have been squeaking. I thought, well, that's an unexpected improvement. But then I happened to look up and saw that it wasn't squeaking because it had fallen off completely. And that turned out to be just the start of the trouble, sir.

The Soldier lights his cigarette using a battered old Zippo lighter.

The Traveller When the other cogs started to come crashing down I thought it would simply stop working, breakdown.

The Soldier It's a glowing testament to the workmanship, sir, that the inscriber carried on in spite of all that.

The Traveller *(His eyes revealing that he is now trapped in the memory of what he's seen)* But it wasn't writing anything. It was just stabbing. Stabbing and stabbing. And that cotton wool thing wasn't rotating the body, it was thrusting it upwards and…

The Soldier All very unfortunate, sir.

The Condemned Man has found The Officer's pitch pipe. He toys with it.

The Traveller It was as if the machine was alive and it was devouring her. *(beat)* No, murdering her. Brutally murdering her in a sick, bloody frenzy.

The Traveller slumps onto the chair.

The Soldier *(Moving in close on the Traveller and standing over him)* Yes, that's what it was like, sir. Very nicely put. You've got a way with words.

The Traveller I wanted to help, I did, but how could I have done anything?

The Soldier Don't reproach yourself, sir. You'd have had to be out of your mind to have gone anywhere near it.

The Traveller I was close enough to see. See things I'll never be able to un-see, never be able to forget.

The Soldier Ain't that the truth.

The Traveller snaps out of his memory and gives The Soldier a confused yet irritated glance.

The Soldier seems oblivious to The Traveller's reaction. He moves away.

The Soldier Anyway, best not dwell on it, sir. It's the sort of thing that could keep you up at night.

The Traveller You should have shut down the whole apparatus.

The Soldier Impossible, sir. Once the needles of the harrow have penetrated flesh it can't be stopped. Everything was automatic and built to run its course.

The Traveller *(With revulsion in his voice)* Run its course?

The Soldier Well, sir. Not like this. Never like this. I'd say that it's damaged beyond repair. But it did manage to fling her body into the pit.

The Traveller shakes his head and begins to put his jacket back on.

The Traveller You'll see to a burial? I think she'd have liked to be buried near the Old Commandant.

The Soldier *(Taking off his jacket)* Well, the pit is near enough for that, sir.

The Traveller What?

The Soldier flings his jacket to the ground and begins rolling up his shirt sleeves.

The Soldier The old man is buried right here. *(He jabs his heel against the ground)* A place in the cemetery was denied him by the Chaplain. And I can't see the Chaplain being any more charitable when it comes to the Officer.

The Traveller *(Looking around in disbelief)* The Old Commandant is buried here?

The Soldier Oh, yes. For ages people couldn't work out where to bury him. Finally, they just buried him here. Of course, *(He plonks into the chair and sits back)* the Officer explained none of that to you. I'm not very surprised, she was the one most ashamed about it. Took it very bad. A few times she even tried to dig up the old man at night, but she was always chased off.

The Condemned Man is rubbing a finger around the bowl. He licks the remains of the rice pudding from his finger.

The Traveller *(Still glancing around at the ground)* But there's no grave stone, nothing to mark where.

The Soldier turns to the table and looks at the leather document folder. He seems too nervous to even touch it. He then glances in the direction of the pit and shrugs. He opens the folder, goes amongst the paperwork and takes out a few sheets. He beckons The Traveller over and spreads one of the sheets out on the table.

The Traveller goes over to join him.

The Condemned Man goes too. He now seems very interested in the documents and immediately starts to handle them.

The Traveller Look, I keep saying, I can't understand these things.

The Soldier This is nothing to do with the apparatus. This is a diagram drawn by The Officer, showing this whole area in every detail, where exactly the old man is buried and how the monument should be built.

The Traveller holds up the document, it looks no different to any of the ones we've seen already – Another labyrinth of dark lines and symbols.

The Soldier *(Handing The Traveller another sheet)* This is the design for the monument itself.

Another incomprehensible mass of hatched lines and symbols is held up.

The Soldier rummages amongst the papers, looking for a particular document. It seems to be missing but then he finds it in the hands of The Condemned Man.

The Soldier Ah, *(He takes the document and hands*

it to The Traveller) And this would have been the inscription.

The Traveller takes the document. This one is smaller than the others but just as impenetrable. He hands it back to The Soldier.

The Traveller Can you read it for me?

The Soldier No. I don't understand them either. But I can tell you exactly what it says. The Officer would read it aloud every morning. Sometimes, over and over. *(He stubs out his cigarette)* She'd have tears in her eyes.

The Soldier clasps the document to his chest mockingly and does not look at it again.

The Soldier "Here rests the once and future Commandant. *(He raises his eyebrows at the Traveller)* His followers, who are now not even permitted to have a name, buried him in this grave and erected this stone. *(He jumps to his feet, mimicking The Officer)* There exists a prophecy that one day the Commandant will rise again! And from this hallowed ground, will lead his followers to a glorious reconquest of the colony. We will be victorious! Have faith and wait!"

The Condemned Man has found The Officer's goggles. He has put them on and is standing to attention.

The Soldier scrunches the document into a ball and tosses it over his shoulder.

The Traveller *(Takes a deep breath, then…)* Can you tell the Commandant that I have become unwell and have decided to return directly to my ship?

The Soldier He'll be very disappointed, sir.

The Traveller He'll get over it. *(He takes one last look around)* I can't imagine he'll have much use for my opinions now.

The Traveller picks up his suitcase and starts to make his exit through the audience.

The Condemned Man tugs at The Soldier's sleeve. They exchange whispers. They both seems to become very excited about something. They nod and smile at each other, then they kiss.

The Soldier *(Calling after him)* Take us with you, sir. He's supposed to be dead. *(He points a thumb at The Condemned Man)* And nobody will miss me for days, I'm assigned to the Officer and well, she's saying nothing. Anyway, they wouldn't dare search or delay the ship of an honoured guest, such as yourself, sir. Take us with you, please?

The Traveller stops and turns.

The Traveller I'm sorry, but I can't. That would be quite impossible.

The Soldier Sir, please?

The Traveller It would do you no good, anyway.
You two would be imprisoned in my country.

He turns his back and continues to leave.

The Traveller Perhaps even sent to a penal colony.

*The Soldier and The Condemned Man silently watch
him go, they are holding hands.*

Lights dim to blackout.

www.ingramcontent.com/pod-product-compliance
Lightning Source LLC
Chambersburg PA
CBHW060050050426
42448CB00011B/2384